Presented to

Caitlin M'Allister

June 2001

Blackmannan Sunday School.

CHRISTIAN ART    TEL: 01323 437700

First published 1992 by Victoria House Publishing,
King's Court, Parsonage Lane, Bath BA1 1ER,
a subsidiary of The Reader's Digest Association, Inc.

Copyright © 1992 Joshua Morris Publishing, Inc.

Reprinted 1994, 1997

British Library Cataloguing-in-Publication Data.
A catalogue record for this book is available from
the British Library.

ISBN 1-85724-837-6

Printed in China.

# My Very First Golden
# BIBLE

As told by the Reverend Dana Forrest Kennedy
Illustrated by Ellen Dolce
Edited by Etta Wilson

Reader's Digest Children's Books

# The Old Testament

# The New Testament

# Introduction

For Christians and Jews, the Bible is the most important book ever written. It tells stories about people – their lives, their hopes, their thoughts. It also tells about God and considers who He is, what He does and how He wants to be involved in our lives.

*My Very First Bible* is a selection of favourite stories from the Bible. The author has followed the New King James version closely. The stories are told in a way that not only brings them vividly to life for young children, but also encourages children to read the Bible for themselves as they grow older.

This book shares the wondrous truth that God loves us and wants us to love Him, too.

The Rt. Reverend Clarence N. Coleridge, Bishop Suffragan
*Episcopal Diocese of Connecticut, USA*

The Reverend Thomas J. Driscoll
*The Catholic Center, Bridgeport, Connecticut, USA*

Rabbi Charles A. Kroloff (for the Old Testament)
*Temple Emanu-El, Westfield, New Jersey, USA*

# Old Testament

# God Made Everything

*In the beginning God created the heavens and the earth.*
*The earth was without form, and void; and darkness was on the face of the deep.*
**Genesis 1:1-2**

In the beginning, the universe was shapeless and empty. Nothing had any form or colour. There were no animals, no birds, no people, no blue sky, no earth, no sun.

God created the earth with oceans and dry land. He made the sun to give light during the day, and the stars to shine at night. God filled the oceans with fishes and the dry land with plants and animals.

Last of all, God made Adam and Eve, and gave them the beautiful garden of Eden.

"Everything in this garden is yours," God said to them, "except the tree of knowledge. You must not eat its fruit."

But a snake in the garden tempted Eve saying, "Eat the fruit. It won't hurt you. It will make you wise."

So, Eve ate the fruit. Then she gave some to Adam, and he ate it, too.

When God found out that Adam and Eve had disobeyed him, He sent them out of the garden of Eden. Then God placed an angel with a flaming sword to guard the entrance to the garden so that they could never return.

# An Angry Brother

*...when they were in the field ...*
*Cain rose against Abel his brother and killed him.*
**Genesis 4:8**

Adam and Eve had two sons, Cain and Abel.
Cain was a farmer and Abel was a shepherd. One
day Cain and Abel both brought offerings to God.
Abel's gift pleased God more than Cain's.

This made Cain angry. He found Abel alone in
a field and killed him.

Later God asked Cain, "Where is your brother?"

Cain answered, "I don't know. Am I my brother's keeper?"

"The ground cries out that you killed your brother," God said. "You have done a terrible thing."

So God punished him. He told Cain that he had to leave his home and wander all over the world. No crops would grow for him, and everyone would know of his sin.

Cain was afraid someone would try to kill him. But God put a special mark on Cain's forehead so that no one would harm him. Cain would have to live with his punishment.

# Noah's Big Boat

*Only Noah and those who were with him in the ark remained alive.*
**Genesis 7: 23**

As time passed, God looked at the world He had made and saw that people were cruel and selfish. There was only one good man named Noah who loved God. One day God said to Noah, "I am going to start again. I will flood the earth with water and destroy every living creature. But, first, I want you to build a big strong boat, an ark.

"Then take two of every kind of animal and bird into the ark. Take two elephants, two monkeys, two leopards, two rabbits, and two ducks – two of every animal, bird and insect in the world. Take all your family and all the creatures into your ark. There you will be safe."

Noah did as God told him. Then it began to rain. It rained for forty days and forty nights.

Water covered the whole world, but Noah's big boat floated on top of the flood waters. At last the rain stopped. The water began to go down. Noah sent out a dove to see if any dry land had appeared. The dove returned with an olive branch in her beak, so Noah knew that they would soon be able to leave the ark.

When the ark came to rest on top of a mountain, God told Noah that he could now take his family off the big boat. So Noah and his family walked onto the dry land with all the animals and birds following after them.

Noah made an altar and worshipped God, thanking Him for saving their lives and for the return of dry land.

God was happy with Noah and put a beautiful rainbow in the sky to show His pleasure.

"This is a sign of my love, " God said. "I promise I will never flood the earth again."

# Abraham's Terrible Test

*...Abraham built an altar there and placed the wood in order;*
*and he bound Isaac his son and laid him on the altar, upon the wood.*
**Genesis 22:9**

Once again, people filled the earth, and among them there was a good man called Abraham. God chose him for a special plan. He promised Abraham He would make a great nation from Abraham's family.

Then God gave a son to Abraham and his wife, Sarah. They named him Isaac.

One day God called to Abraham, "Abraham, take Isaac your only son whom you love so much. Go into the wilderness and sacrifice him to Me."

Usually Abraham would kill a lamb and offer it to God. Must he kill his son this time? The thought of this made Abraham very sad, but he knew he must obey God. The next morning Abraham loaded his donkey and set out with Isaac.

Isaac did not understand what was happening.
"Where is the lamb that we are going to sacrifice?"
he asked his father.

Abraham replied, "God will give us one."

Then Abraham built an altar. He put Isaac on
top of the altar. Slowly, he took out his knife.

Just then a voice from heaven called out, "Stop! Don't hurt the boy. I now know you love Me because you obeyed My voice."

Just then Abraham saw a ram caught in the nearby bushes.

Instead of his son, Abraham sacrificed the ram and offered it to God. God was pleased.

# Rebekah At The Well

*...there was Rebekah, coming out with her pitcher on her shoulder...*
**Genesis 24:45**

Abraham was growing old, and before he died he wanted to find the right wife for his son Isaac. So he sent a trusted servant back to the place where he had come from. Abraham believed that God would help his servant find a wife for Isaac.

When the servant came to the town, he went to its well where women came to get water. He asked God to let the first one to give water to him and his animals be the woman he was looking for. Soon, he saw the beautiful Rebekah coming to the well with her pitcher on her shoulder.

The servant asked Rebekah for a drink. She not only gave him water, but also brought some for his animals. He knew this was God's sign.

The servant then asked Rebekah's family if she could go back with him to marry Isaac. "Yes ," they said. "This is what God wants." The servant was so thankful that he bowed down and praised God.

Then Rebekah went back with the servant to Isaac's home. She became Isaac's wife and he loved her.

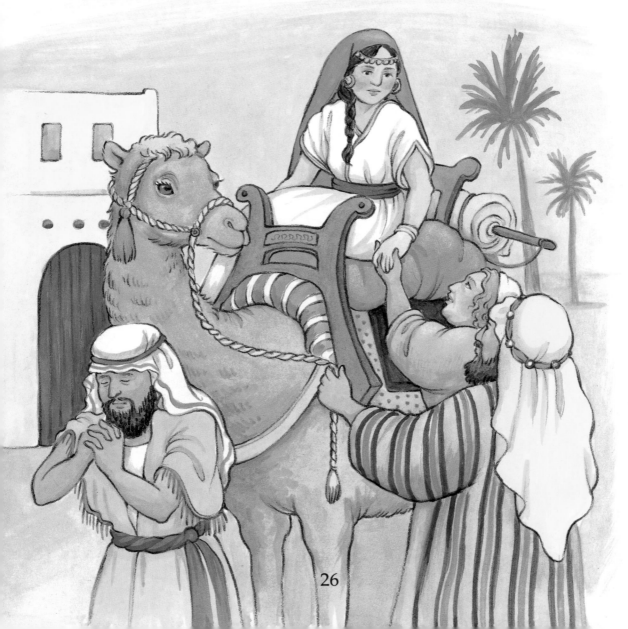

# Joseph's Coat Of Many Colours

*Now Jacob loved Joseph more than all his children...*
*he made him a tunic of many colours.*
**Genesis 37:3**

After Isaac and Rebekah married, they had a son named Jacob. When Jacob grew up he had twelve sons. He loved them all, but he loved Joseph the most. He made Joseph a beautiful coat of many colours. The gift made Joseph's brothers jealous and angry.

One day Jacob sent Joseph out to visit his brothers who were working in the fields far from home. When Joseph found his brothers, they took his beautiful coat from him and sold him to a band of traders who were going to Egypt.

Then the brothers dipped Joseph's coat in
goat's blood and took it home to show their father.
  "It is Joseph's coat," Jacob said. "He must have
been killed by wild animals." Jacob was very sad.
He did not know that his son was alive and that
they would be reunited some day.

# Pharaoh's Mysterious Dreams

*And Pharaoh said to Joseph, "I have dreamed a dream...*
*I have heard it said of you that you can understand a dream, to interpret it."*
**Genesis 41:15**

The traders took Joseph with them into Egypt, where they sold him again. Later he was thrown in jail with Pharaoh's butler and baker. Both men had mysterious dreams which God helped Joseph to explain. When the butler was released from prison, Joseph said, "Tell Pharaoh about me, and help me get free."

Some time later, Pharaoh had two strange dreams. The butler told Pharaoh about Joseph, and Pharaoh sent for him.

"I have dreamed that seven fat cows were eaten up by seven lean ones," Pharaoh said. "Then I dreamed that seven plump stalks of grain were eaten up by seven thin stalks. Can you tell me what this means?"

"There will be seven years of plenty followed by seven years of famine," Joseph said. "Egypt must prepare."

Pharaoh was so impressed with Joseph's wisdom that he made him the keeper of Egypt's grain.

Sure enough, after seven years of plenty there came a great famine. Joseph's brothers became so hungry that they came to Egypt to buy food from Pharaoh's grain keeper.

When Joseph told them who he was, his brothers were afraid. They thought he would punish them for selling him long ago, but Joseph had forgiven them.

"Don't be afraid," Joseph told his brothers. "God sent me into Egypt to save lives." Joseph embraced his brothers and gave them food. Soon he brought his father and all his brothers to Egypt to live with him.

# Moses Among The Bulrushes

*...she took an ark of bulrushes for him,*
*...put the child in it, and laid it in the reeds by the river's bank.*
**Exodus 2:3**

Moses was a beautiful baby boy. His parents were descendants of Abraham, Isaac and Jacob. They were called the Children of Israel and they were living in Egypt. A wicked pharaoh did not like the Children of Israel. He forced them to be slaves and wanted all their boy babies killed. Moses's mother had a plan to save her son. She put him in a basket among the bulrushes at the river's edge.

Moses's sister, Miriam, stood in the rushes to watch the basket. Soon it floated near the king's daughter who came to the river to bathe. She heard the baby crying and peered into the bulrushes. There was little Moses in the basket.

"He is an Israelite baby," she said. "I must save him. I will keep him for my own."

"Would you like me to find someone to nurse the baby for you?" asked Miriam.

"Yes," the Princess said.

So Miriam brought the baby home to their mother who took care of him. When Moses was old enough, he went to live at the Princess's house and became her son. Even though Moses was not with his own people, God never stopped watching over him.

# An Amazing Fire

*Then Moses said, "I will now turn aside
and see this great sight, why the bush does not burn."*
**Exodus 3:3**

One day as Moses was leading his flock of sheep along the side of a mountain, he came upon a bush that was on fire. Moses went closer and saw a strange sight. The bush was not being consumed by the flames!

"Take off your shoes," said a voice from the burning bush. "You are on holy ground."

"Who speaks?" asked Moses.

"I am the God of Abraham," the voice answered. "I want you to go to Pharaoh and tell him to let the Children of Israel go free."

"I can't do that," said Moses. "Pharaoh won't listen to me."

"You can do it with My help," said God. "You will use your shepherd's staff to show Pharaoh that I have sent you. Throw your staff on the ground."

Moses followed God's instructions. When he threw down the staff it turned into a snake. When he picked it up, it became a staff again.

Moses knew that God would help him, so he set off for Egypt to ask Pharaoh to let his people go.

# The Great Escape

*...and the waters were divided. So the children of Israel went
into the midst of the sea on the dry ground, and the waters
were a wall to them on their right hand and on their left.*
**Exodus 14:21, 22**

With God's help, Moses tried many things to
help his people escape from Egypt. But Pharaoh
would not let the Children of Israel go. He
wanted to keep them as his slaves.

Finally, God said to Moses, "I will try one
more thing to help you. Have your people put a
spot of lamb's blood over their doors tonight.
Every house so marked will be safe. Tell them to
pack up, eat a quick supper, and be ready to leave
in a hurry."

39

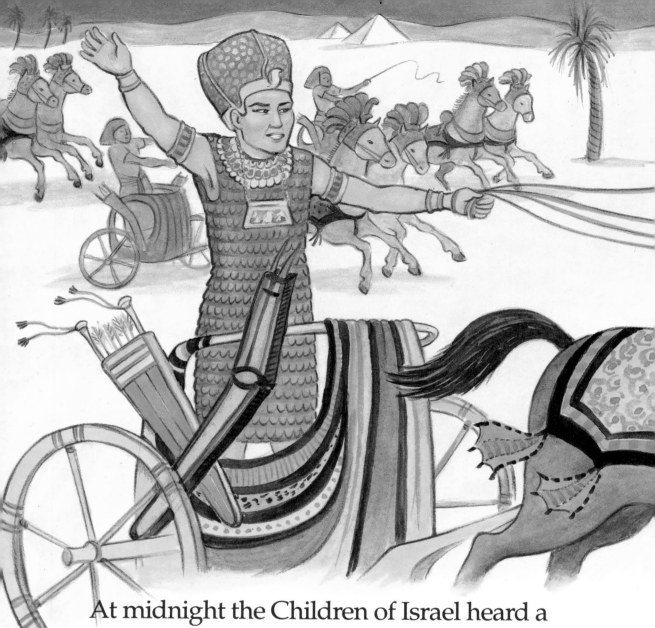

At midnight the Children of Israel heard a loud crying coming from the homes of the Egyptians. The oldest son in every Egyptian home was dead, even Pharaoh's son. Pharaoh finally decided to let the Children of Israel go.

But they had not gone far when Pharaoh changed his mind. He chased after them with soldiers in chariots pulled by fast horses.

The Children of Israel ran until they came to the Red Sea. There was no way to cross. They were trapped!

"Stand firm," said Moses, "and see how God will help you." Moses stretched out his hand over the sea, and God pushed the water out of the way so that they could cross.

The Children of Israel walked on a dry path through the sea. But when the Egyptians tried to follow, the walls of water fell in on the soldiers and their horses and drowned them. At last the Children of Israel were free. God had saved them!

# Rules From Above

*Moses...was there with the Lord forty days and nights...
He wrote on the tablets the words of the covenant,
the Ten Commandments.*
**Exodus 34:27, 28**

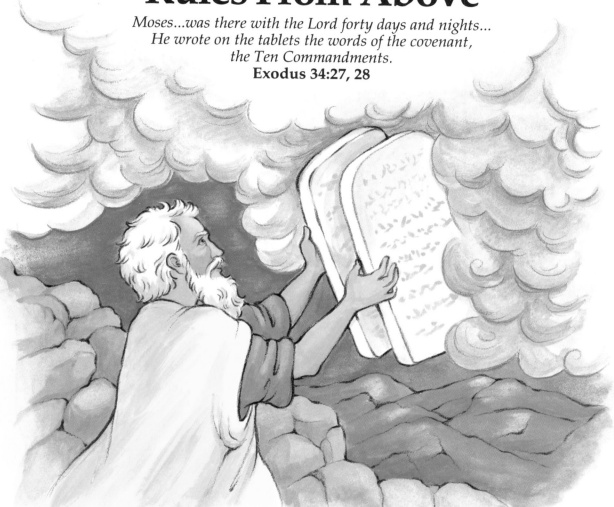

After the Children of Israel had wandered in the desert for many days, they came to a high mountain.

God told Moses to climb the mountain, and there He gave him ten rules carved into two stone tablets. "These are My Commandments," God said to Moses. "I want all My people to obey them."

Moses took the tablets and went back down the mountain. There he found the Children of Israel worshipping a golden statue of a calf. In a rage, Moses threw down the stone tablets, and they broke into pieces.

When the people realized that worshipping an
idol was wrong, they were sorry. Moses said he
would ask God to forgive them. Moses went back
up the mountain, where God again wrote the
rules on two new stones.

"Keep My Commandments," said God, "and I
will give you a new land."

When Moses came down from the mountain,
his face glowed. He gave the people the new
tablets and told them always to follow God's laws.

# The Walls That Fell Down

*...when the people heard the sound of the trumpet, and the people shouted with a great shout, ...the wall fell down flat.*
**Joshua 6:20**

After Moses died, God chose Joshua to lead the Children of Israel into the land of Canaan, which He had promised them. Two things stood in their way, the Jordan River and the city of Jericho.

At the Jordan River Joshua told the priests carrying the Ark – the special box containing God's laws – to lead their people into the river. As soon as the priests' feet touched the water, God drew the river back so the Children of Israel could walk across on dry land.

Then, they had to face the soldiers of Jericho. "Joshua," God said, "march your people around the city walls for seven days. Carry the Ark with you. On the seventh day have the priests blow one long note on their horns. At the same time, have everyone give a loud shout."

The Children of Israel did what Joshua told
them to do. On the seventh day, when the priests
blew their horns, the people gave a loud shout,
and the walls of Jericho came tumbling down!
The city was theirs!

# A Surprise Haircut

*If I am shaven, then my strength will leave me,*
*and I shall become weak, and be like any other man.*
**Judges 16:17**

Among the Israelites was a very strong young man named Samson. Once, a thousand Philistines tried to kill Samson, but he picked up a big bone and killed them all.

The Philistines wanted to stop Samson. They hated him because of his strength and because of his faith in God. The Philistines asked Delilah to help them. Samson loved and trusted Delilah even though she was a Philistine.

When Delilah asked Samson what made him so strong, he answered her truthfully. "If someone cut my hair, I would not be strong anymore."

That night, after Samson fell asleep, Delilah cut his hair. Then the Philistines easily tied Samson up, blinded him, and threw him into prison. But as time passed, Samson's hair grew long again.

When the Philistines later brought Samson to a big feast to mock his weakness, Samson asked a servant to help him put his hands on two pillars that held up the building's roof. Then Samson prayed to God for strength and pushed on the pillars as hard as he could.

The pillars broke and the roof fell in, killing everyone. Samson's last prayer was answered.

# How Gideon Beat The Enemy

*Then they blew the trumpets and broke the jars...
and shouted, "A sword for the Lord and for Gideon."*
**Judges 7:19,20**

For many years the Children of Israel had been
ruled by the Midianites.

One day as Gideon was working in his
father's fields, an angel came to him and said,
"The Lord is with you and He will help you
defeat the Midianites."

Gideon selected an army of 300 men. They planned to trick the Midianites during an attack at night. Each Israelite soldier carried a light covered by a pitcher in his left hand and a trumpet in his right hand. When the time came, Gideon and all his soldiers blew their trumpets and broke their pitchers, letting their lights shine. Then they all shouted loudly, "For the Lord and for Gideon!"

Scared by the noise and the light, the Midianites ran in every direction. Gideon and his soldiers chased them right out of the country.

"Gideon, be our king," the Children of
Israel begged.

"No," replied Gideon. "God will be your king!
Obey Him."

So, the Midianites were beaten and, for as
long as Gideon lived, there was peace in the land
of Israel.

# God Speaks To The Boy, Samuel

*Then the Lord came and stood and*
*called as at other times, "Samuel, Samuel!"*
**I Samuel 3:10**

Year after year a woman named Hannah prayed for a child. When she finally had a baby boy, Hannah was very happy. She named the child Samuel and promised God that Samuel would always serve Him.

While Samuel was still very young, Hannah took him to live at the Temple. A priest named Eli became his teacher.

One night in the Temple, Samuel woke up because he heard someone calling his name. He ran to Eli and said, "Here I am."

"I did not call you," Eli replied. "Go back to bed."

This happened three times. Finally, Eli realized that it was God who was calling the boy. Eli told Samuel to answer God and listen carefully to what God had to say.

Later that night God called again. "Samuel, Samuel," He said.

Samuel answered, "Here I am, Lord."

God told Samuel that He had chosen him as a prophet. Over the years, God told Samuel many things, all of which came true. As he grew older, Samuel kept listening to God, and people trusted him.

# David Fights A Giant

*So David prevailed over the Philistine with a sling and a stone, and struck the Philistine and killed him.*
**I Samuel 17:50**

In the time of King Saul, the Philistines attacked the Israelites. The armies fought for many weeks and no end was in sight. Then a giant Philistine soldier named Goliath dared any Israelite soldier to fight with him.

"If he kills me," said Goliath, "Israel wins. If I kill him, the Philistines win." But Goliath was so big, no Israelite soldier dared to fight.

A young shepherd named David heard
about Goliath's dare, and told King Saul,
"I will fight him."

"You are much too young," said the king.

"God has helped me kill the lion and the bear
who attack the sheep," David said. "He will help
me now." The king granted him permission.

David went to a brook and picked up five smooth stones. Then he ran to meet Goliath.

When Goliath saw that David was only a boy, he made fun of David. "I will feed you to the birds," he called.

"You think you can kill me with your sword or spear," said David. "But God will help me kill you."

Then David took a stone from his bag, placed it in his slingshot, and aimed it at the giant. The stone hit Goliath's forehead, and the giant fell down dead.

When the Israelites saw Goliath fall, they cheered loudly and chased the Philistine army out of Israel.

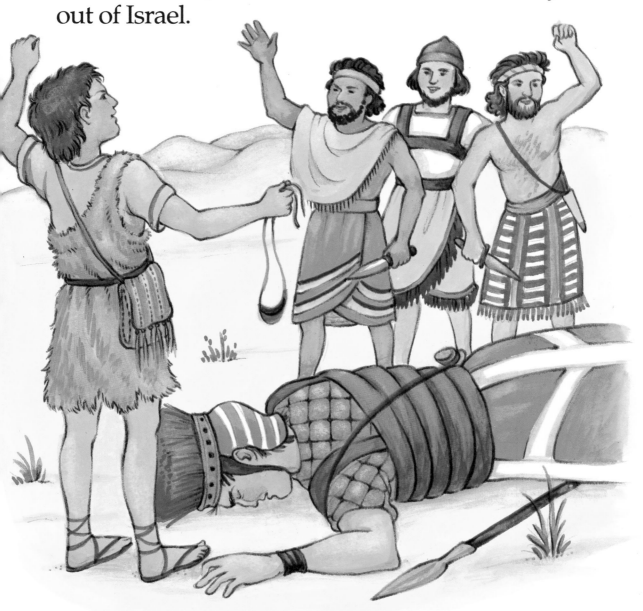

# A Shepherd's Song

*The Lord is my shepherd; I shall not want.*
**Psalm 23:1**

The Children of Israel often sang when they worshipped God. They sang to remember happy times. They sang to comfort each other in times of trouble. They sang songs telling of God's greatness, and they sang songs asking for God's help.

The Children of Israel put all their songs together in a book called the "Psalms."

Many of the psalms were written by David, who became a great king of Israel. But before he was a king, David was a simple shepherd. He liked to sing to God while he was tending his sheep. One of his songs is Psalm 23.

"The Lord is my shepherd; I shall not want. He makes me lie down in green pastures; He leads me beside still waters. He restores my soul; He leads me in the paths of righteousness for His name's sake.

"Yea, though I walk through the valley of
the shadow of death, I will fear no evil; for You
are with me; Your rod and Your staff, they
comfort me.

"You prepare a table before me in the presence of my enemies. You anoint my head with oil; my cup runs over.

"Surely goodness and mercy shall follow me all the days of my life; and I will dwell in the house of the Lord forever."

# A Wise King

*So the king answered and said, "Give the first woman the living child, and by no means kill him; she is his mother."*
**I Kings 3:27**

Davidʼs son, Solomon, ruled after him as king of Israel. God made Solomon very wise. From far and near, people came to seek his advice.

Once, two women came to King Solomonʼs court. Each one claimed to be the mother of a baby boy. They were angry and argued loudly before the king.

When they finished speaking, Solomon asked that a sword be brought to him. "Cut the baby in two," he ordered, "and give half of the baby to one woman, and half to the other."

When she heard these words, one of the two women cried out in horror, "No, no don't do that! Let the baby be given to the other woman. I do not want my child killed."

But the other woman replied, "No, let the baby be neither yours nor mine. It is only fair to divide it."

Solomon knew then that the woman who did not want the baby harmed was the real mother. "Do not kill the child," he said, "but give it to this good woman. She is the baby's mother."

When the people heard about the king's decision, they knew that Solomon had truly been blessed with the wisdom of God.

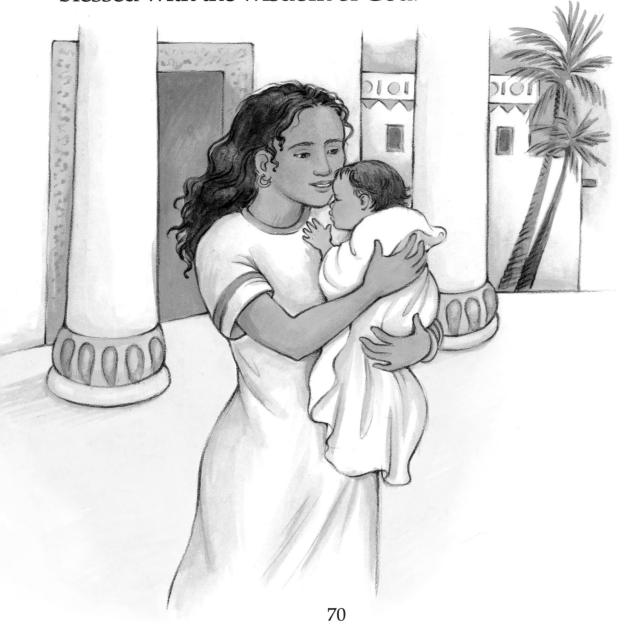

# A Mountain-Top House For God

*Then Solomon determined to build a temple for the name of the Lord, and a royal house for himself.*
**2 Chronicles 2:1**

When King Solomon's father David was king, he had started gathering supplies to build a magnificent Temple where his people could worship God. But God had told David not to build the Temple. David was a soldier, and God wanted His Temple to be built by a man of peace. So God told David that his son Solomon would build the Temple.

Now that Solomon was king, he decided to finish his father's work. He hired many men. They carried logs and gold and silver up the mountain. It took seven years to build the great Temple.

Finally the Temple was ready. It was the most beautiful building anyone had ever seen. The priests brought the Ark into the most holy place in the Temple.

God was pleased with the Temple that Solomon had built. He let His spirit enter the building so that all the people could see that it was His house.

The people were glad. They sang and danced and worshipped God in His Temple. Solomon was pleased with the Temple, too. He was happy that he had fulfilled his father's dream.

# God's Prophet Elijah

*...Elijah said...,"How long will you falter between two opinions?*
*If the Lord is God follow Him; but if Baal, then follow him."*
**I Kings 18:21**

Many years after King Solomon, a wicked king named Ahab and his wife, Jezebel, ruled over Israel. They made false gods out of stone and metal and prayed to them. God sent his prophet Elijah to warn King Ahab that what he was doing was wrong.

"You have displeased God," Elijah told the king. "There will be no rain in Israel until I say so."

This made the king very angry, and Elijah was afraid. God told Elijah to hide in the wilderness near a brook where God took care of him. Every day ravens brought Elijah bread and meat to eat.

But there was no rain, and before long the
brook dried up. God then told Elijah to go and
live with a poor widow and her son. She had only
a little bit of food left.

"Share your bread with me," said Elijah. "God
will give you all the food you need until it rains."

Elijah stayed safely in the widow's house for
three years. Then God told him to go and see
King Ahab again.

So Elijah went back to King Ahab. "You must choose between the false god Baal and the Lord our God," he said. "It will not rain until you do."

Elijah also told Ahab to call all the prophets of Baal to the top of Mount Carmel. The people of Israel came too.

"Let us have a contest," Elijah said. "Let Baal's prophets build an altar and place dry wood and meat on it for an offering. But do not light the fire. I will do the same thing.

"Then let Baal's prophets pray to Baal, and I will pray to God. The god who sends fire is the true God."

The people thought this was a good test.

The prophets of Baal prayed and shouted and danced around their god's altar all day long, but nothing happened.

Then Elijah called the people to come close and watch. He made an altar, and put the dry wood and meat upon it. Then he dug a trench around it. Last of all, he had the people pour water over the altar.

They poured so much water that it filled the trench around the altar. Then Elijah prayed to God.

In a flash, fire came down from the sky. It burned up everything, even the water in the trench.

The people fell to the ground. "The Lord is God," they shouted.

"God will now send rain," said Elijah. Before long it began raining, and the great drought came to an end.

# The Prophet's Cloak

*He also took up the mantle of Elijah that had fallen from him, and went back and stood by the bank of the Jordan.*
**2 Kings 2:13**

The time had come for Elijah the prophet to go to heaven. On that day he and his friend Elisha went walking by the River Jordan.

Soon they decided to cross the river. So Elijah took off his coat and struck the water with it. At once, the waters parted to make a path. The two men crossed to the other side without even getting their feet wet.

Then Elijah asked his friend Elisha what he might like to have from him.

Elisha replied, "Please let me be a prophet like you are."

"If you see me ascend to heaven," said Elijah, "you will have your wish."

Just then a chariot of fire drawn by fiery horses came down from above. A whirlwind swirled round and round and carried Elijah up to heaven.

With wonder, Elisha watched his friend ascend
to heaven. He picked up Elijah's coat, which had
fallen to the ground, and went back to the river.
Then Elisha struck the water with the coat. Some
water went left, and some went right. Elisha
walked across the river on a dry path!

On the far side of the river, a large group of
men stood watching. "You have Elijah's spirit,"
they said to Elisha. "You are now God's prophet."
Elisha's wish had been granted.

# The Prophet's Warnings

*...they let Jeremiah down with ropes. And in the dungeon there was no water, but mire. So Jeremiah sank in the mire.*
**Jeremiah 38:6**

In a part of Israel called Judah, there lived a man named Jeremiah. God spoke to him and said, "Before you were born, I set you apart to tell people about Me."

"I do not know how to talk to people," answered Jeremiah. "I am too young."

God said, "Say what I tell you to say and you will be all right."

After that, Jeremiah told people about God all his long life. Sometimes they listened, and sometimes they didn't.

He told King Josiah and the people of Judah, "God is upset with you. You do not obey His rules."

So King Josiah made his people live by God's rules and God was pleased.

Later, Zedekiah became king. He wanted his soldiers to fight the Babylonian army, which was attacking Judah. Jeremiah warned the king not to fight.

The king didn't like what Jeremiah said. He tried to silence Jeremiah by putting him into a deep well.

But a palace worker took some ropes and pulled Jeremiah to safety.

After that, King Nebuchadnezzar of Babylon destroyed the city of Jerusalem. His soldiers tore down the Temple and carried many of the Israelites off to Babylonia.

Jeremiah tried to comfort the people. He told them about God's promises. "One day God will bring you back to Jerusalem. He will send you a fair and good king from David's family, and you will love God in a new and better way."

# The Handwriting
# On The Wall

*...the fingers of a man's hand appeared and wrote*
*... on the wall of the king's palace.*
**Daniel 5:5**

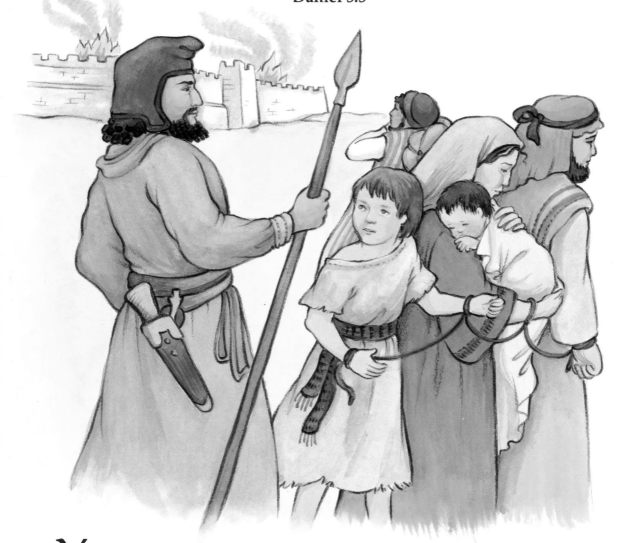

Young Daniel was one of the Children of Israel captured and carried off to Babylon. Daniel lived as a helper in the king's palace and learned many new ideas, but he never stopped loving God.

Several years later, Belshazzar, the king of Babylon, gave a party. At the party he drank out of the gold and silver cups his father had stolen from God's Temple in Jerusalem.

Suddenly a hand appeared in the air and wrote four strange words on the wall: "MENE, MENE, TEKEL, UPHARSIN."

The king was so frightened that his knees knocked. He called all his wise men to tell him what the words meant, but they could not. They told him to call Daniel.

"God sent the hand," Daniel said to the king. "It was wrong to drink out of the cups from God's Temple. You are a wicked king, and your rule is about to end."

That very night, King Belshazzar was killed and a new king took over.

# Daniel In The Lion's Den

*So the king gave the command, and they brought Daniel and cast him into the den of lions.*
**Daniel 6:16**

Daniel became an important leader under Darius, the new king of Babylon. This made the other leaders jealous. They wanted to get rid of Daniel. They knew how much Daniel loved God, so they convinced King Darius to make a new law. The law said everyone must pray only to the king.

Daniel knew it was a trick, but he would not pray to the king. Three times a day he prayed to God before his window. The bad men were watching. When they told King Darius, he was very upset. But Daniel had broken the law.

That night Daniel was thrown into a den of hungry lions.

Early the next morning, the king ran to the lions' den. "Daniel, has your God saved you?" he called.

"Yes, my God sent an angel to shut the mouths of the lions. He has kept me safe," Daniel replied.

King Darius was pleased. He took Daniel out of the lions' den and had the bad men thrown to the hungry lions instead.

Then the king made a new law. It said, "Everyone in my kingdom must worship Daniel's God."

# Swallowed By A Big Fish

*Now the Lord had prepared a great fish to swallow Jonah.*
*And Jonah was in the belly of the fish three days and three nights.*
**Jonah 1:17**

God once spoke to a man named Jonah, saying, "Go to the city of Nineveh and warn its people that if they don't start following my laws, I will punish them."

Jonah did not want to go to Nineveh. So he boarded a ship and tried to run away. But God caused a terrible storm. Jonah asked the sailors to throw him into the sea. He thought God was trying to punish him for running away. A big fish swallowed Jonah and brought him back to land.

God spoke again to Jonah, telling him to go to Nineveh with His message. This time Jonah went at once.

When he reached the great city of Nineveh, Jonah spoke to the king and people. He told them, "God is going to destroy your city because you don't follow His laws." The king and people were very sorry and afraid. They promised to be good and obey God.

God was pleased and He forgave them.

Now Jonah was angry. He didn't think that the people of Nineveh deserved to be spared. Jonah made himself a shelter outside the city and waited to see what would happen.

While Jonah waited, God made a tree grow next to him to protect him from the hot sun. Jonah was happy to see the tree.

Then God killed the tree and made the sun hotter than ever. Jonah grew angry again.

"Are you angry because the tree which I gave you died?" asked God.

"Yes, very angry," replied Jonah.

God said, "If you are sorry for a little tree, why should not I be sorry for the great city of Nineveh? It has thousands of innocent people living in it!"

At last Jonah understood God's mercy.

# New Testament

# His Name Is Jesus

*And she will bring forth a Son, and you shall call His name Jesus,*
*for He will save His people from their sins.*
**Matthew 1:21**

Long ago in the little town of Bethlehem in Judea, Jesus was born. His mother, Mary, and Joseph, her husband, had arrived in the town on the very night Jesus was to be born.

They went to the inn to find a room. The innkeeper told them, "There are no rooms left, but you may stay in the stable."

That night, with only Joseph and the animals nearby, Mary gave birth to a son. Joseph named the child Jesus.

While Jesus lay asleep in a manger, some shepherds arrived. "The angels came and sang to us," they said to Joseph and Mary. "They told us that our saviour had just been born. They showed us where to find the baby."

Later, three wise men came. They had travelled a great distance.

"This baby was born to be King of the Jews," they said. "We followed his star from the East; it led us here."

Then they knelt down and gave Jesus their presents of gold, frankincense and myrrh.

All the people in the stable were happy because they saw the baby Jesus.

# His Father's Business

*"Did you not know that I must be about My Father's business?"*
**Luke 2:49**

When he was twelve years old, Jesus went with his family to visit the Temple in Jerusalem. After the visit, his parents and all his family started for home. They had travelled a full day's journey towards Nazareth before Mary and Joseph discovered Jesus was not with them.

Mary and Joseph hurried back to Jerusalem where they spent three days looking for Jesus. Finally they found him in the Temple. He was sitting with the teachers, listening and asking questions. Everyone was surprised by how much he knew!

"We have been worried," said Mary.

Jesus answered, "Didn't you know that I would be in my Father's house?" His answer puzzled his mother, but she was glad Jesus was safe.

Jesus went back home with his parents. He grew bigger and wiser and became much loved by all who knew him.

# God Is Pleased

*Then a voice came from heaven,*
*"You are My beloved Son, in whom I am well pleased."*
**Mark 1:11**

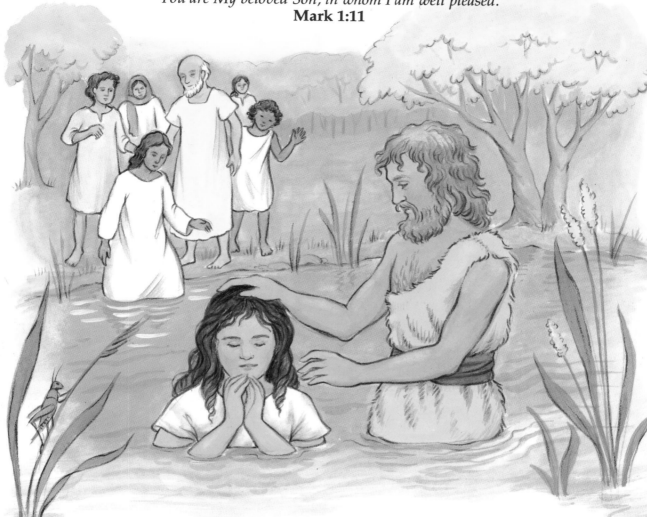

John the Baptist was a prophet who lived near Jerusalem. He ate grasshoppers and wild honey. His clothes were made of camel's hair, and he always wore a big leather belt.

John was very wise. Many people came to hear him preach. He baptized them in the Jordan River.

One day Jesus came and asked John to baptize him. John did not want to, because he knew that Jesus was wiser and more holy.

"You should baptize me," he said to Jesus.

But Jesus said it was right for John to baptize him.

So John baptized Jesus in the river. When Jesus rose out of the water, the sky opened and the Spirit of God, like a dove, came down to him. At the same time, a voice from heaven said, "You are my own dear Son. I am very pleased with you."

# The Devil At Work

*Then Jesus was led up by the Spirit
into the wilderness to be tempted by the devil.*
**Matthew 4:1**

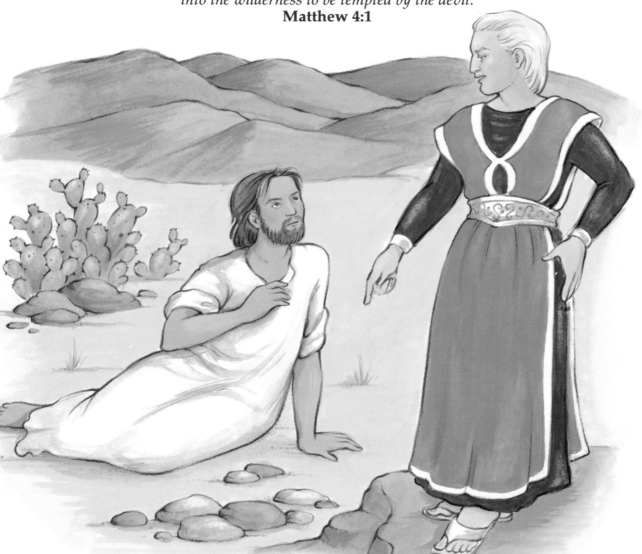

After his baptism, Jesus was sent by God out into a lonely desert for forty days and forty nights. Jesus did not eat or drink. The devil came to Jesus and said, "If you are God's son, turn these rocks into bread. Then you will have food."

Jesus replied, "It takes more than food to live. Man must obey God's rules."

Then the devil set Jesus on the very top of the Temple. "Jump off," the devil said. "God will not let you get hurt."

"It is wrong to test God's love," Jesus answered.

Finally, the devil took Jesus to a tall mountain from which Jesus could see the whole world and all its riches. "If you will bow down and serve me, I will give all this to you," the devil said.

"Get away from me, devil!" Jesus said. "God is the only one I will worship and obey."

So the devil left him, and angels came to care for Jesus.

# Going Fishing

*"Do not be afraid. From now on you will catch men."*
**Luke 5:10**

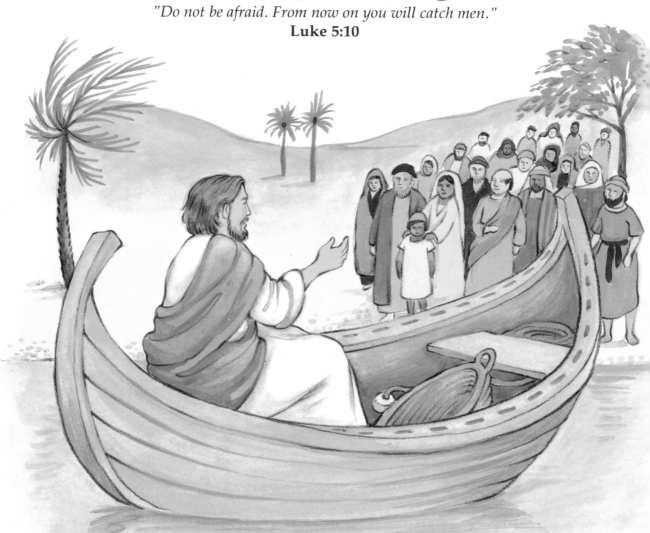

One day Jesus went down to the shore of Lake Galilee. A crowd had gathered to hear him tell them about God.

Jesus got into the boat of a fisherman named Peter and taught the people standing on the shore.

When he finished speaking, Jesus said to Peter, "You and James, John and I are all going fishing."

"It is useless," Peter answered. "We fished all night and caught nothing. But, if you say so, we'll go."

The fishermen caught so many fish that their nets broke. Fish filled the boats and the weight almost sank them.

The fishermen couldn't believe their eyes. Peter was frightened. The other fishermen were, too. Jesus said, "Do not be afraid. From now on, instead of bringing fish into your boats, you will help me bring people into God's Kingdom."

The fishermen pulled their boats out of the
water and left them on the shore. They left their
family and their friends. They left everything to
follow Jesus. They became Jesus's first disciples.

# The Loaves And Fishes

*"There is a lad here who has five barley loaves and two small fish..."*
**John 6:9**

Once thousands of people went out into the countryside to hear Jesus. It grew late, and Jesus saw that the people were tired and hungry. So he asked his disciples, "How can we feed all these people?"

Philip replied, "We do not have enough money to buy food for everyone."

Just then Andrew said, "There is a young boy here who has five loaves of barley bread and two small fishes. But that is not enough to feed so many people."

Jesus told his disciples, "Tell the people to sit down."

So everyone sat on the grass. Then Jesus thanked God for the barley bread and handed the loaves to the people. Then he blessed the fishes and handed them out as well.

When everyone had eaten as much as they
wanted, there was still plenty left over! Then
Jesus said to his disciples, "Pick up what remains.
Let's not waste even a bit."

They filled twelve baskets with leftover bread!
It was a miracle.

# Come, Little Children

*"...Let the little children come to Me, and do not forbid them;
for of such is the kingdom of God."*
**Mark 10:14**

Some mothers and fathers heard what Jesus was
saying about God's love. They wanted Jesus to
bless their children. So they brought their families
– boys and girls and even babies – to the place
where Jesus was teaching.

The parents pushed their way through the crowd to bring their children before Jesus. But the disciples tried to stop them. The disciples thought that Jesus should not be bothered by children. He was too busy.

When Jesus saw what was happening, he spoke sternly to his disciples. "Let the little children come to me, and do not stop them. Unless you love and trust God the way a little child does, you cannot get into God's kingdom."

Then Jesus picked up the children and placed his hand on their heads. He gave his blessing to each and every one of them.

# The Little Lost Sheep

*"Rejoice with me, for I have found my sheep which was lost!"*
**Luke 15:6**

Crowds of thieves and other people who had done bad things came to hear Jesus talk. The leaders and teachers murmured against Jesus and his listeners. So Jesus told them this story:

"If anyone has a big flock of sheep," Jesus said, "and even one sheep is missing, what happens? The shepherd leaves the flock and looks until he finds the one lost sheep.

"When he finds it, he picks up the tired sheep and carries it home.

"Then the shepherd calls to friends and neighbours to celebrate. 'Rejoice with me,' he says. 'I have found the lost sheep.'

"It is like that in heaven," Jesus said. "The angels are happy for the good people who always love God, but they are even happier when a person who has strayed from righteous ways starts to love God."

# The Prodigal Son

*...the younger son gathered all together, journeyed to a far country,*
*and there wasted his possessions with prodigal living.*
**Luke 15:13**

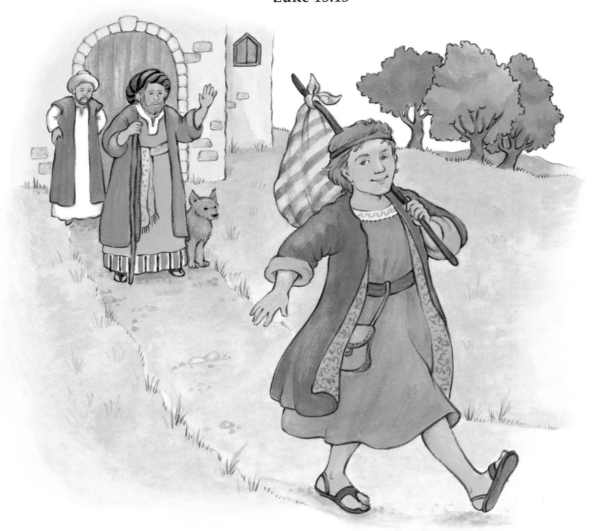

Jesus told his followers a story: "Once there was a rich man who had two sons. When they grew up, the older son stayed home to help his father. But the younger son wanted to go away and have fun.

"So the father gave this son half his wealth, and the young man spent it all foolishly. He was so hungry, he had to take a job looking after pigs. He even ate what the pigs ate.

"Then he thought, 'Back home, my father's servants are treated far better than I am here. I will go home. Maybe my father will let me be one of his servants.'

"When his father saw him coming, he was so happy, he hurried out to meet his younger son. He told his servants, 'Dress him in new clothes. Put a ring on his finger and shoes on his feet.' That night the father gave a party for him.

"The older brother was angry. 'It isn't fair,' he complained. 'I have obeyed you all these years, but you never gave a party for me.'

" 'My son,' his father replied, 'your brother was lost and now he is found. Don't be angry. Let's all be glad.'

"God is like that father," Jesus said. "He rejoices when someone returns to Him."

# Make Way For The King

*... a great multitude...took branches of palm trees and went out to meet Him, and cried out: "Hosanna!..."*
**John 12: 12,13**

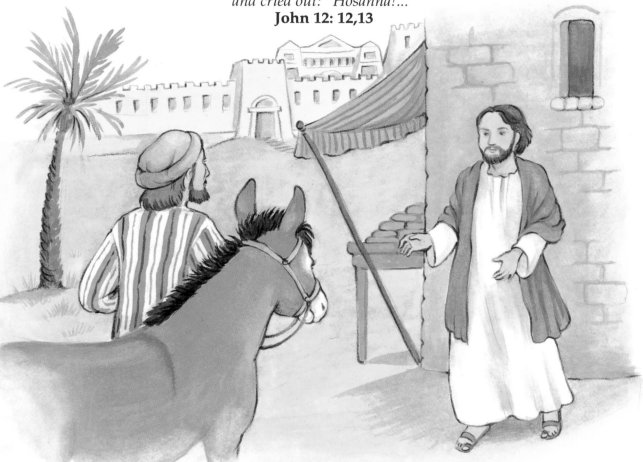

It was Passover! Everyone who could went to Jerusalem for the celebration.

Jesus got ready to go, too. He asked his disciples to get a donkey for him and told them just where to find it.

"Untie it and bring it to me. Tell anyone who asks what you are doing, 'Our master needs it,'" Jesus said.

The disciples did as he asked. Then they laid their coats on the young donkey's back, and Jesus got on it.

Their trip to the city was exciting. People laid palm branches in Jesus's path. Some even spread their coats on the road for the donkey to walk on.

"Hosanna! Praise God!" they shouted. "Blessed is he who comes in the name of the Lord! Bless the King of Israel!"

In Jerusalem, Jesus went to the Temple. There he found money changers and animal sellers cheating the people who came to worship God. Jesus overturned their money tables. He let their animals and birds go free.

"God's house is for praying to God," Jesus
cried. "You have made it a den of thieves."

After that, Jesus came to the Temple every day
to teach. The leaders did not like this. But the
people were eager to learn from Jesus.

# A Good-Bye Meal

*And when the hour had come, He sat down, and the twelve apostles with Him.*
**Luke 22:14**

At Passover, Jesus and his twelve disciples took their places at the table. They were going to celebrate together.

Jesus picked up a piece of bread and broke it. As he passed the pieces, he said, "This is my body. Whenever you eat it, think of me."

After that he poured wine into a cup. He gave
it to his disciples and said, "This is God's new
promise to you, sealed with my blood.
Remember me when you drink it."

The disciples did not know what Jesus meant,
but they gladly shared the bread and wine.

While they were eating, Jesus said, "The one I now hand the bread to is going to turn me over to my enemies to be killed." He gave the bread to Judas, who took it and left the table. Then, Judas went out into the night.

After the meal, Jesus took a bowl of water and washed and wiped his disciples' feet. "Do you understand why I am doing this?" he asked. They were not sure.

So Jesus told his disciples, "You must love one another as I have loved you. Then everyone will know you are my disciples."

Then they sang a song of praise and went out to the Hill of Olives.

# God's Will Be Done

*"...nevertheless, not what I will, but what You will."*
**Mark 14:36**

After the Passover supper Jesus went into the Garden of Gethsemane, which was on the Hill of Olives. Peter, James and John were with him. But Jesus left them and went alone to a big rock to pray. His friends fell asleep.

Kneeling by the rock, Jesus talked with God. "Please God," he prayed, "I do not want to be killed." But he ended his prayer, "I will do what You want, not what I want."

When he finished his prayer, Jesus woke up his friends. "Let us go," he said. "Everything is settled."

As Jesus and his friends were leaving the garden, Judas and some soldiers stopped them. Judas said to the soldiers, "The one I kiss is Jesus. Arrest him." Judas went up to Jesus and kissed him. The soldiers seized Jesus and took him away.

Jesus's friends were all afraid. They ran away. All except Peter who followed some way behind Jesus and the soldiers. When anyone asked Peter if he was one of Jesus's followers, he pretended not to know Jesus.

Then the soldiers led Jesus across a yard. As Jesus passed by Peter, he looked him straight in the eye. At that moment a cock crowed. Peter remembered how Jesus had said, "Before the cock crows, Peter, you will say you do not know me."

"I have failed Jesus," thought Peter. He was so ashamed of himself that he cried and cried. He was very sad.

# Three Crosses On A Lonely Hill

*Then two robbers were crucified with Him,*
*one on the right and another on the left.*
**Matthew 27:38**

Early in the morning, the Roman soldiers brought Jesus to the leaders of the people.

"Are you the Son of God?" the leaders asked.

"I am," replied Jesus.

"That can't be true!" the men shouted. "You must die for saying such a thing."

So the leaders took Jesus to Pontius Pilate, the Roman governor. Pilate did not think Jesus was guilty of any crime. He asked the crowd what he should do with Jesus.

"Crucify him," they shouted.

So Pilate ordered that Jesus be killed. Then Pilate washed his hands and said, "Don't blame me for Jesus's death."

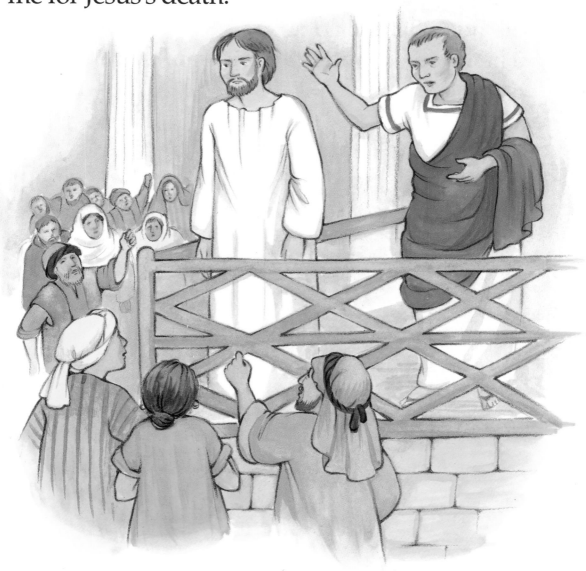

The soldiers put a crown of thorns on Jesus's head. They played a cruel game, pretending that he was a king.

Afterwards they made Jesus carry a heavy cross through the streets to Calvary Hill. There, they nailed him and two thieves on crosses.

Jesus looked down from his cross at the people. "Father, forgive them," he prayed. "They know not what they do."

Then he died, and his spirit went up to God.

Joseph of Arimathea buried Jesus in a small cave cut into rock on the side of a hill. He rolled a big round rock in front of the tomb to shut it.

Mary Magdalene and another woman named Mary watched while Joseph buried Jesus.

Then Joseph and the two Marys returned to their homes. It had been a very sad day, but there would be happier days to come.

# Love Wins

*"...Do not be afraid, for I know that you seek Jesus who was crucified.*
*He is not here; for He is risen, as He said."*
**Matthew 28:5, 6**

On Sunday morning, several women who were Jesus's followers went to the place where Jesus was buried. But when they got there the big stone had been rolled away, and the tomb was empty!

Then they saw an angel who said to them, "Jesus is not here. He is alive."

The women ran back to tell the news. The disciples rushed to the tomb. It was true. Jesus's body was gone!

That same Sunday, two of Jesus's disciples were walking along the road to Emmaus. They were talking about Jesus and how he had been killed.

Jesus joined them on the road, but they did not recognize him. He told them how the prophets had said Jesus would live again.

They asked the man to have supper with them. When he broke the bread, they knew he was Jesus! The two disciples were very happy. They hurried back to Jerusalem to tell the others that Jesus was alive.

Later that same night, the disciples were all together. Suddenly, Jesus was there in the room with them! "Peace be with you," he said. "As God sent me, I am sending you. Tell all the world about God's love."

Then he blessed them and rose up to Heaven. The disciples prayed and celebrated. Then they went out among the people to tell of Jesus and all his teachings.

# Fire Dancing Overhead

*Then there appeared to them divided tongues,
as of fire, and one sat upon each of them.*
**Acts 2:3**

One holiday, Jesus's friends all met together.
Suddenly they heard a sound like a great rushing
wind. The sound filled the whole house.

Next a burning flame came down on the head
of each person, and they were all filled with God's
Spirit. They began to speak so that people from
every country could understand what they
were saying.

People heard about this miracle, and soon a big crowd had gathered in front of the house. Peter went outside to tell them that Jesus was the promised one from God. He had died, but God made him alive again.

"We have received God's Spirit," Peter said. "And Jesus can help you receive Him, too."

"What must we do?" the people asked.

"You must tell God you are sorry for whatever wrongs you may have done. Then you must be baptized in Jesus's name. God will fill you with His Spirit."

Three thousand people were baptized that very day.

# New Sight For Saul

*Then he fell to the ground and heard a voice saying to him,*
*"Saul, Saul, why are you persecuting me?"*
*Acts 9:4*

A man named Saul thought Jesus's followers were saying things against God. One day Saul and his friends set out for Damascus to capture some of Jesus's followers and put them in jail.

As they travelled along the road, a bright light flashed like lightning out of the sky. Saul fell to the ground.

"Saul, Saul, why are you trying to harm me?" a voice called.

"Who are you?" asked Saul.

"I am Jesus," came the answer.

Saul trembled with fear and asked, "What is it you want me to do?"

Jesus told him to go on to Damascus and there he would learn what to do next.

When Saul stood up, he found he could not see. His friends led him to Damascus. There, Jesus sent a follower named Ananias to heal Saul's blindness and to baptize him.

Saul, who was later called Paul, became a changed man after that. He spent the rest of his life teaching people about Jesus.

# John's Heavenly Vision

*I, John...was in the Spirit on the Lord's Day...*
**Revelation 1:9,10**

John, who was a disciple, told other people about Jesus. The leaders did not like this, and John was sent away to the island of Patmos. One day when he was old and full of God's Spirit, John had a vision.

In this vision, John saw God sitting on a great throne in heaven. Twenty-four holy people dressed in white robes, with golden crowns on their heads, sat praising God. In the centre was a Lamb that had, like Jesus, been killed. Thousands of angels came to sing their praises to God and the Lamb.

John also saw a beautiful city coming down from heaven to take the place of Jerusalem. The streets of this new city were paved with gold, and its gates were made of precious pearls.

A loud voice from the throne said to John, "God will live with the people in this city. Its gates will always be open and everyone will be happy."

Then Jesus spoke and said, "I am coming soon."

And John was glad that Jesus would be coming again. He said, "Amen! Come Lord Jesus."